THE BATTLE OF THE BULGE

Nazi Germany's Final Attack on the Western Front

BY MICHAEL BURGAN

Richard Bell, PhD
Associate Professor of History
University of Maryland, College Park

CAPSTONE PRESS
a capstone imprint

Tangled History is published by Capstone Press,
1710 Roe Crest Drive, North Mankato, Minnesota 56003
www.capstonepub.com

Library of Congress Cataloging-in-Publication Data
Names: Burgan, Michael, author.
Title: The Battle of the Bulge : Nazi Germany's Final Attack on the Western
    Front / by Michael Burgan.
Description: North Mankato, Minnesota : Capstone Press, 2020. | Series:
    Tangled history | Includes bibliographical references and index. |
    Audience: Grade 4 to 6. | Audience: Age 8 to 12.
Identifiers: LCCN 2019006032| ISBN 9781543572599 (hardcover) | ISBN
    9781543575590 (paperback) | ISBN 9781543572636 (eBook pdf
Subjects: LCSH: Ardennes, Battle of the, 1944-1945—Juvenile literature
Classification: LCC D756.5.A7 B86 2020 | DDC 940.54/219348—dc23
LC record available at https://lccn.loc.gov/2019006032

Summary: In narrative nonfiction format, follows people who experienced the
Battle of the Bulge during World War II.

Editorial Credits
Christopher Harbo, editor; Kazuko Collins, designer; Eric Gohl, media
researcher; Laura Manthe, production specialist

Photo Credits
Alamy: Chronicle, 50, 95, Photo 12, 85, 99, PJF Military Collection, 23, 49,
Sueddeutsche Zeitung Photo, 8, 15; Capstone: 79; Getty Images: Bettmann,
32, Heinrich Hoffmann, 12, Historical, 29, 65, 83, US Army, 53; Library
of Congress: 42, 58, 92; National Archives and Records Administration:
cover, 4, 17, 19, 68, 70, 75, 77, 88, 101; Newscom: akg-images, 61, Everett
Collection, 47, Heritage Images/Art Media, 80, Photoshot/War, 102, US
Army/Atlas Photo Archive, 35, ZUMA Press/Keystone Pictures USA, 26;
Shutterstock: defotoberg, 104; SuperStock: Pantheon/Illustrated London
News Ltd, 39, 44; Wikimedia: Public Domain, 6, 105

Printed and bound in the United States of America.
PA70

TABLE OF CONTENTS

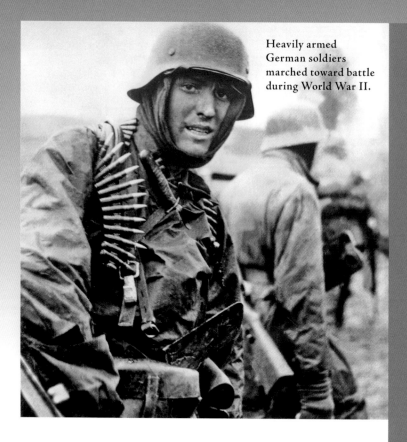

Heavily armed German soldiers marched toward battle during World War II.

FOREWORD

Starting on September 1, 1939, German leader Adolf Hitler unleashed his military might across Europe. He wanted to control as much of the continent as he could. Hitler and the members of his ruling Nazi Party thought they were part of a "master race" that had a right to rule over other Europeans. Hitler had an especially strong hatred for Jewish people. He blamed German Jewish people for the country's loss of World War I (1914–1918) and for many of its problems after the war.

United States President Franklin D. Roosevelt opposed Hitler and the Nazis. But after taking part in the last year of World War I, many Americans did not want to fight in another war. On December 7, 1941, though, war came to the United States. Germany's ally, Japan, attacked the U.S. naval base at Pearl Harbor, in Hawaii. Within days, the United States joined the Allied forces of Great Britain, Canada, and several other nations already battling the Axis powers of Germany, Japan, and Italy.

As some U.S. forces fought the Japanese on islands across the Pacific, Roosevelt made plans to fight the Nazis in Europe. The goal was to land troops in France and push the Germans out of the countries they had conquered.

Planning for that massive invasion took two years. Finally, on June 6, 1944, U.S. and other Allied

Allied forces landed on the beaches of Normandy, France, during the
D-Day invasion on June 6, 1944.

troops landed on the beaches of Normandy, France.
The attack was called D-Day, and the Allies had
assembled a huge fighting force. They had almost
5,000 ships and boats of all sizes, along with about
13,000 aircraft.

On the first day of the invasion, more than
160,000 troops stormed ashore. The Germans had
been expecting an attack, but they could not hold

off the Allies. In the weeks that followed, more Allied troops landed in Normandy, along with a steady stream of supplies. Through the summer and fall of that year, the Allies drove almost all of the German forces out of France.

By December 1944, U.S. military experts were confident they could soon defeat the German forces in Western Europe. Allied forces were in Belgium and Luxembourg, close to the German border. At the same time, the Soviet Union, another U.S. ally, was pushing back German forces in the eastern half of Europe.

Still, even as Germany fought a war on two fronts, Hitler was not ready to give up. As early as September, the German leader had already started thinking about launching a massive attack of his own. He was determined to stop the Allied advance toward his country. Although his troops faced fierce fighting in the east, Hitler did not think the Soviets would launch another major offensive there until early in 1945. That gave him time, he thought, to strike the Allies in the west. The planning for a huge counterattack began.

1

German Lieutenant Colonel Otto Skorzeny

BEFORE THE ATTACK

Lieutenant Colonel Otto Skorzeny arrived for his meeting with Adolf Hitler. Skorzeny had just completed a successful mission in Hungary and had received orders to meet Hitler at his bunker. The building, and several others close by, was known as the Wolf's Lair. Hitler had built these bomb-proof buildings in an eastern part of Germany called Prussia, where he felt safe from enemy attacks.

Skorzeny knew Hitler liked and trusted him. Besides the Hungarian operation, the lieutenant colonel had carried out a daring mission in 1943. Skorzeny and his men rescued Italian leader Benito Mussolini after he had been captured by Italians who opposed his rule. Mussolini was Hitler's closest ally in Europe.

Now, in the Wolf's Lair, Skorzeny listened as Hitler said, "I have perhaps the most important job in your life for you."

The officer heard Hitler outline his plan for the great counterattack that would begin in the Ardennes, a forested region of Belgium and neighboring Luxembourg. Hitler said that new planes powered by rocket engines would take part in the attack.

But Hitler was not just counting on weapons to win the battle. He needed deception too. Hitler asked Skorzeny to lead a small group of English-speaking commandos. He promised to give Skorzeny the uniforms of captured British and U.S. soldiers, as well as Allied weapons and vehicles, to use in the mission. Once the men crossed enemy lines, Hitler said, "You can cause the greatest confusion among the Allies by giving false orders and upsetting their communications."

Skorzeny told Hitler that he doubted he had enough time to train his men for a mission like this.

Hitler admitted that he was asking a lot of Skorzeny. "But you must do all that is humanly possible," he said.

Adolf Hitler

Adolf Hitler welcomed generals Siegfried Westphal and Hans Krebs into his map-filled bunker. The two generals had barely entered the room when they were ordered to sign a statement. Hitler told the officers that what they were about to hear was top secret. He warned them that if they talked about it to anyone, they would be shot.

The generals and other officers present signed the statement. Then Hitler told them that more German forces would be moving to the Western Front in several weeks.

After a while, Hitler met privately with Westphal and Krebs. They listened as Hitler outlined a military operation he called *Wacht am Rhein*—German for "Watch on the Rhine." The Rhine was the major river in western Germany. If the Allies did somehow learn of this plan, Hitler wanted them to think he was merely preparing to defend Germany from the advancing Allied armies.

Adolf Hitler (seated center) and his military leaders reviewed plans for the Watch on the Rhine offensive.

Instead, Hitler had come up with a plan for a huge offensive operation.

Hitler was convinced that he could gather enough of his forces to defeat Allied troops along the Meuse River in Belgium. Then the Germans would split the British and U.S. forces. That way, they could not help each other as Hitler's troops tried to hold on to the Belgian port city of Antwerp. The Allies were hoping to use the city to bring supplies to their troops. Hitler counted on a swift victory, which might convince the Allies to end the war, rather than keep fighting and invade Germany.

Westphal and Krebs did not command the soldiers that would go into battle. They worked for Field Marshals Gerd von Rundstedt and Walther Model, who commanded many of the troops expected to carry out Hitler's plans. Hitler told the two men to go back to Rundstedt and Model and assure them that they would have plenty of new troops. He explained that he hoped to launch the attack on November 25, when a forecast of bad weather would keep Allied planes on the ground. And the secrecy surrounding the plan would be the key to its success. Hitler counted on surprising the Allies before they knew what had hit them.

Lieutenant Colonel Otto Skorzeny

Prussia, Germany,
November and early December 1944

In the days that followed his meeting with Hitler, Lieutenant Colonel Skorzeny realized this mission was almost impossible. Not enough of his men spoke English well, and he didn't have all the Allied equipment he needed. But Skorzeny continued preparing his men for their part in the Watch on the Rhine.

Toward the end of November, he met with the officers who would command the troops in Belgium. Skorzeny explained that their goal was to capture several bridges behind enemy lines. After the meeting, a lieutenant came to talk to him.

"Sir, I believe I know the real objective of the brigade. We are to go straight to Paris and capture Allied headquarters!"

Skorzeny was surprised and amused. He had heard nothing about this and assumed the lieutenant

Otto Skorzeny (left) met with Adolf Hitler to receive the Knight's Cross award for rescuing Italian leader Benito Mussolini in 1943.

was creating his own plan. He said, "Well, go and think it all over very carefully and work out the details."

Going into December, Skorzeny wondered when the attack would come. It had been delayed until December 1 and then postponed again, as the German military struggled to get all the troops in place. Skorzeny met with Hitler several times. At one meeting, Hitler told him he could not enter enemy territory with his troops. The leader feared Skorzeny could be captured and taken prisoner. He did not want to lose the services of one of his best officers.

Skorzeny was disappointed to hear this. But he knew it would not be wise to challenge Hitler's order.

General Dwight D. Eisenhower

Maastricht, the Netherlands,
December 7, 1944

U.S. General Dwight D. Eisenhower arrived in Maastricht, in the Netherlands, from Luxembourg, where he had met with one of his top generals, Omar Bradley. Bradley and Eisenhower were now going to discuss with other Allied generals their strategy

U.S. General Dwight D. Eisenhower

to defeat Adolf Hitler and the Nazis. Since 1942, Eisenhower had commanded U.S. troops fighting in Europe. Then, in December 1943, he became the commander of all the Allied troops that carried out the D-Day attack in France on June 6, 1944. Now Eisenhower's job was to lead those men to victory by defeating the Nazis once and for all.

Eisenhower wanted to seize the Ruhr Valley, a part of western Germany that produced most of the country's steel. That would keep Hitler from rebuilding his military as the Allies destroyed tanks, planes, and artillery. But as Eisenhower learned in his meeting at Maastricht, not all the generals under him agreed with his plans.

Field Marshal Bernard Montgomery of Great Britain led troops stationed along the northern part of the Allies's 450-mile front. Montgomery asked Eisenhower for more troops to cross the Rhine River and attack the Germans there. Montgomery was convinced that one mighty blow could cripple the Nazis.

Eisenhower respected "Monty," as he was known. But he did not like how the British general always wanted more troops under his command. Eisenhower rejected his plan. He explained that he wanted to keep U.S. General George S. Patton Jr.'s 3rd Army in the south and strike along a larger part of the front.

Great Britain's Field Marshal Bernard Montgomery

Eisenhower had first laid out this strategy months before. He was not willing to change it. To prepare for a broad attack, he had stationed most of the Allied troops north and south of the Ardennes forest in eastern Belgium. He did not need to keep many men there, he thought, because the Germans were not likely to want to fight on such difficult terrain.

Besides, Eisenhower doubted the Germans would attack at all. British intelligence had broken a secret German code and often knew Hitler's plans. There was no sign that Germany was planning an attack. Most of the intelligence suggested that Germany was preparing to defend itself against a major Allied attack away from the Ardennes.

After the Maastricht meeting, Eisenhower continued to make plans for the invasion of Germany. Starting on December 19, Patton's troops would attack an area of Germany called the Saar. Eisenhower hoped to weaken the Germans there so they could not resist the Allied attack over the Rhine and into the Ruhr Valley.

Adolf Hitler

Adolf Hitler held the first of two meetings with his generals in Ziegenberg, Germany. The town was near the Rhine River, and his headquarters there were called the Eagle's Eyrie, or nest. From the outside, the buildings looked like typical German homes. But they were made with concrete walls three feet thick, and armed soldiers and antiaircraft guns guarded the site.

As the generals listened, Hitler explained the importance of the attack that was only days away. He read from a script he had written out beforehand. At times, his hands trembled. Hitler told the officers, "If a few really heavy blows were inflicted [then the Allies's unity] could suddenly collapse with a huge clap of thunder."

The next day, Hitler gave his speech again to other officers. He still had not announced when the attack would come, but everyone knew it would be soon. He said, "There is no turning back; if things go wrong, we shall be in for hard times. We must attack and start a war of movement once more."

Each of the generals there had one minute to speak. General Josef "Sepp" Dietrich took his turn. He and Hitler were old friends, and Dietrich had been faithful to him for more than 20 years. Now he commanded the 6th Panzer Army. This force of Panzer tanks and men had been formed just for Watch on the Rhine. Hitler asked Dietrich if his army was ready.

"Not for an offensive," the general replied. He told Hitler that he needed more ammunition and more fuel.

"You are never satisfied," Hitler said. He told Dietrich and the other generals that they would have what they needed to defeat the enemy.

U.S. Lieutenant Lyle Bouck

Lanzerath, Belgium,
December 15, 1944

U.S. Lieutenant Lyle Bouck looked out through the darkness. Ice and snow weighed down the tree branches that surrounded him. More snow

U.S. Lieutenant Lyle Bouck

could come at any time, during what was turning out to be a harsh winter. Bouck had told his entire platoon to stay awake that night. Their commander in the 99th Division, Major Robert Kriz, had said U.S. troops might be launching an attack soon, and the Germans might try to counterattack in force. Bouck wanted his men to be ready for anything.

Bouck's group had settled into its position just outside the village of Lanzerath, Belgium, less than a week before. Kriz had explained that there was a gap in the U.S. forces in this part of the Ardennes forest. He wanted Bouck and some of his men to fill it until reinforcements arrived. Bouck was not happy to hear this and knew his men would not be thrilled either. They were trained to gather intelligence, not actively fight the Germans. But Bouck trusted Kriz when he said it was just a temporary move.

So Bouck's men had gone into Lanzerath, in an area the Americans called the Ghost Front. Since the Ardennes was so thick, Allied commanders thought they could safely keep only a small number of troops in this 85-mile stretch of the front. Bouck's platoon took cover in foxholes other U.S. troops had dug before. For added protection, they hacked down trees and placed the logs over the top of the holes.

Now, as midnight approached, several of the men came to see Bouck. They described hearing noises in the darkness. Bouck listened and then had radioman James Fort send a message to the regiment's headquarters: "Platoon members reported hearing enemy vehicle noises. They believed the sounds they heard were noises caused by . . . heavy tracked vehicles, such as tanks, on a highway in enemy territory."

The Germans were up to something, but Bouck did not know what.

2

German Colonel Jochen Peiper

THE FIRST DAY

With dawn approaching, Colonel Jochen Peiper prepared to address his troops. He was part of Nazi Germany's most elite fighting force, the SS. He had won several medals for his bravery during the war, and he knew he was one of Hitler's favorite officers.

Peiper had learned just two days before that his battle group of more than 100 tanks, large artillery pieces, and about 5,000 men was supposed to race more than 60 miles west to the Meuse River. They would guard the river crossings so more Germans could march toward Hitler's main target of Antwerp, Belgium, which the Allies now controlled.

When he received his orders, Peiper was not happy. "These roads were not for tanks, but were for bicycles," he told his commanders. Peiper had been told that the orders came from Hitler, and he was expected to obey them.

Now Peiper gave his own orders. He told his men they must move quickly. They could ignore small groups of enemy soldiers. They had just one goal—to reach the Meuse as quickly as possible.

Peiper then headed for the command post of Major General Gerhard Engel's 12th Infantry Division. From there, he would watch the opening moments of Germany's attack on the Allied lines. And soon after, he would lead his own troops into battle.

German Sergeant Erich Michely

Near the Germany-Luxembourg border, December 16, 1944, 5:30 a.m.

Sergeant Erich Michely and his men knew something was finally going to happen. Michely had just received word that their division—the 352nd division—would attack that morning. So would other German troops now camped east of the Our River, just outside Luxembourg.

For weeks, Michely and his men had trained with a new artillery gun the German army had just introduced. Altogether, seven men operated the

Spirits ran high among German soldiers on the move in the early stages of the Battle of the Bulge.

gun, with Michely in charge of finding targets and helping his men aim. The gun was pulled by a team of four horses. Michely was in charge of them too.

The sergeant did not know what to expect as he and his men prepared to move out. Earlier in the war, he had fought in Russia, and he had been wounded there that March. After that, he had convinced doctors he could not fight in the infantry anymore. That led to his new assignment with the artillery. He was glad to be a little farther away from enemy fire.

In the days leading up to this morning, Michely and the others knew some big attack was being planned. They had moved ammunition closer to the border and cleared paths for an advance.

Now, at 5:30 a.m. on December 16, the attack was about to begin.

With a mist filling the air and dark clouds overhead, Michely heard large guns begin to pummel enemy forces on the other side of the river. His horse-drawn artillery was too small to take part in this first barrage. But as German troops swarmed out of their camps and crossed the Our River between Germany and Luxembourg, he and his men would have a chance to help their country achieve a great victory.

U.S. Lieutenant Lyle Bouck

Lanzerath, Belgium,
December 16, 1944, 5:30 a.m.

As 5:30 a.m. approached, Lieutenant Bouck sat in the small cabin that served as his command post near his men's foxholes. Suddenly he heard German shells exploding all around him. One landed near his cabin, and he could hear shells ripping through the trees. Looking outside, he could see shrapnel from the trees raining down on the men in their foxholes.

The shelling went on for 90 minutes. Slowly the men climbed out of their holes. All of them had survived the attack. Bouck radioed Major Kriz, who told him to go into town and set up an observation post. He told Bouck that there had been attacks all along the front.

German soldiers charged across a road as they pushed the front line deeper into Belgium and Luxembourg.

It did not take long for Bouck and several of his men to set up a post on the second floor of a home in Lanzerath. Bouck looked out the window. Fog hid the rising sun. Then, through the gray, Bouck saw hundreds of Germans heading their way.

German Colonel Jochen Peiper

Schnee Eifel, Germany,
December 16, 1944, 2 p.m.

While some troops advanced from their position in Germany, Colonel Peiper fumed. A planned jump of German paratroopers had been delayed, and now a massive traffic jam prevented him from leaving Schnee Eifel and sending his tanks to their target in Belgium.

Peiper impatiently asked another officer what the problem was. The officer explained that German troops had earlier blown up a bridge that Peiper's tanks now needed to cross. Despite the setback, Peiper was determined to reach the Meuse as quickly as possible. When his tanks were finally ready to move, he told his men, "Push through rapidly and . . . run down anything in the road ruthlessly."

U.S. Lieutenant Lyle Bouck

Lanzerath, Belgium,
December 16, 1944

As the Germans poured into the village, Bouck and his men ran back to their camp outside of Lanzerath. Bouck called the regiment's headquarters. He told them that as many as 500 Germans were closing in on Lanzerath. The soldier on the other end told Bouck he must be seeing things.

"Don't tell me what I can't see!" Bouck roared. "Bring down some artillery, all the artillery you can."

Bouck waited to hear U.S. gunfire aimed at the advancing Germans, but it never came. He called headquarters again and asked what he and his men should do. This time he was told, "Stay! You are to hold at all costs."

Bouck realized that his small force of about 20 men would have to fight the several hundred Germans he now saw coming his way.

"Fire!" Bouck ordered, and his men began cutting down the Germans slowly advancing toward their position. He watched as Private Bill James scrambled

U.S. soldiers took cover from enemy fire in the wooded Ardennes region of Belgium.

out of his hole and ran to a jeep equipped with a .50 mm machine gun. James began firing. *They're so young*, Bouck thought, watching the Germans die. But so were most of his men. Bouck was only 20 himself. His birthday would be the next day—if he survived.

The attack was over quickly. Bouck was soaked with sweat as he scanned the hill below him. There were dead and dying Germans everywhere.

"Check your holes and see whether we have wounded," Bouck told Sergeant Bill Slape. He soon learned that everyone had survived, although Private Joseph McConnell had been shot in the left shoulder. But he was conscious and still able to fight. Bouck was relieved. He figured he would need all the firepower he had, since the Germans were likely to attack again.

Bouck and his men did not have to wait long. Around 11 a.m., more Germans approached the U.S. position. Once again, Bouck and the platoon cut down the enemy soldiers before they could do any damage. In the afternoon, a third wave of Germans advanced, and the result was the same. Bouck and his men forced the enemy to retreat, leaving more dead German soldiers on the hill. But Bouck knew his troops could not hold out much longer. They were running out of ammunition. He got on the radio to ask again for help.

As he explained that the Germans had surrounded them, a sharp, cracking noise erupted in the lieutenant's ear. A German sniper had shot the phone right out of his hand, and with another shot, destroyed the radio too. Bouck and his men were now completely isolated on the snowy hillside, with Germans all around them.

As night approached, the Germans came at them again. This time Bouck and his men could not fight them off. Groups of German soldiers approached each foxhole and ordered the U.S. troops out. As Bouck tried to communicate with the German officer in front of him, a bullet tore through his left leg. After falling to the ground in pain, Bouck was able to tighten a strap around his leg to stop the bleeding. Then the Germans motioned for him and his men to march. They were now prisoners of war (POWs).

Adolf Hitler

Eagle's Eyrie, Ziegenberg, Germany, December 16, 1944

In his bunker, surrounded by maps, Adolf Hitler listened to his top military aide, General Alfred Jodl, describe the first few hours of Watch on the Rhine. Jodl had good news.

"Surprise had been completely achieved," he said. "The best indication was that no reinforcements were made . . . before the attack."

Hitler was pleased. He could only hope that the rest of his plan worked. He had counted on General Eisenhower wasting time by consulting with President Roosevelt and other Allied leaders. Only then, Hitler assumed, would the Allies respond. Hitler hoped his troops would be well on their way to Antwerp by then.

German Colonel Jochen Peiper

Moving through Belgium,
December 16, 1944

By late afternoon, Colonel Peiper's 1st SS Panzer Regiment was finally underway. His car took the lead as the tanks and men approached the blown-up bridge. He told his driver to go along the river and look for another place to cross. Finally Peiper saw a spot where the regiment could safely cross.

Just before midnight, Peiper reached Lanzerath. He met Colonel Helmut von Hoffman, who commanded the troops that had taken the village.

German foot soldiers got a lift from a Tiger heavy tank during the Battle of the Bulge.

Hoffman told Peiper that there were Americans scattered throughout the forest, and "it was impossible to attack under these circumstances."

Peiper grew angry. All his plans for reaching the Meuse River that day had been smashed, and he was behind schedule. He asked if Hoffman had scouted the area for himself. Hoffman said no—he had relied on the reports of others. Peiper said he would take some of Hoffman's men the next day and lead an attack himself.

German Lieutenant Colonel Otto Skorzeny

Near the Belgian border,
December 16, 1944

Through the morning, Lieutenant Colonel Skorzeny and other officers near the front began to get the first reports of the attack. The first wave of their fellow German soldiers was not advancing as quickly as planned.

Skorzeny's men had their own problems with Operation Greif, the code name for the mission. Without enough Allied equipment, he had sent only several dozen men into enemy territory. Their goal was to carry out sabotage and spread rumors of the strength of the German force. They also planted the rumor that the Nazis planned to race to Paris and try to capture General Eisenhower. While the men who spoke the best English went to work, the rest of Skorzeny's force were traveling with Colonel Peiper's Panzers.

By the end of the day, though, Skorzeny learned that his commandos were having some success. One team had reached the Meuse River. Another team had convinced U.S. artillery to detour away from the front, saying that the Germans had blocked the way. Skorzeny saw for himself some of the damage the Germans were inflicting. As he rode to a new command post, closer to the Belgian border, he spotted the burned-out remains of three U.S. tanks.

That evening, Skorzeny met with several other commanding officers, including General Sepp Dietrich. Dietrich told Skorenzy that the Americans were putting up stiff resistance.

As Skorzeny heard the reports, he realized that even with their surprise attack, the Germans were in trouble. And he doubted how much success Operation Greif would have.

General Dwight D. Eisenhower

Paris, France,
December 16, 1944, 5 p.m.

What had started out as a quiet day quickly turned chaotic for General Eisenhower. Earlier he

General Dwight D. Eisenhower (left) and General Omar Bradley

had spent time at his headquarters writing letters, before leaving to attend the wedding of one of the sergeants on his staff. In the late afternoon, he met with General Bradley to discuss plans for new attacks on the Germans. Now, around 5 p.m., Major General Kenneth Strong entered the room. The British officer was in charge of gathering intelligence for Eisenhower and his staff.

Strong said that they were getting reports from Belgium and Luxembourg of German attacks at several locations along the front. Eisenhower and the other officers debated what it meant. Bradley thought it was just a spoiling attack—a Nazi effort to throw off the Allies before they launched their own offensive.

"That's no spoiling attack," Eisenhower said. He believed the Germans were now on the offensive in the Ardennes.

By midnight on December 16, Eisenhower and Bradley realized the attack was larger than they had first thought. Early the next morning, Eisenhower cancelled the planned Allied attacks so he could rush troops and artillery to cut off the German advance.

3

A German soldier stood beside a disabled American half-track as he sent signals to his fellow soldiers during the initial days of the Battle of the Bulge.

THE BATTLE GOES ON

German Colonel Jochen Peiper

"Let's go!"

Colonel Peiper was eager to advance. Along with the men he had taken from Colonel Hoffman, Peiper left Lanzerath and headed for Honsfeld, Belgium. The Americans they met along the way did not have the firepower to stop the Panzers and other German tanks, and soon Peiper was rolling through Honsfeld. In the village, they found most of the Americans asleep. Peiper's men quickly took 300 prisoners and captured vehicles and antitank guns. Despite some later U.S. resistance, Peiper took Honsfeld. True to his orders, he sped on as more German troops arrived to hold the town.

Even with his success, Peiper was not happy. He desperately needed fuel for his tanks and trucks. He had heard reports that the Allies had a command post in Buellingen, Belgium. The town was bound to have fuel supplies, so Peiper ordered his men to head there.

The 1st Panzer Division reached the enemy outpost and roared in with all its guns firing. Once again, the Americans were not ready to fight back. Peiper ordered the prisoners he took there to fuel his tanks and trucks. When that was done, Peiper rolled on, heading west toward Malmedy, Belgium, on his way to the Meuse River.

U.S. Lieutenant Lyle Bouck

Lanzerath, Belgium,
December 17, 1944

Lieutenant Bouck heard the sound of advancing German tanks in the distance—but he was more concerned with what was in front of him. The Germans had taken Bouck and his men to a small café in the village. Some of the Americans were wounded, including Private James. The Germans indicated that the badly wounded, like James, would be taken out of Lanzerath by truck. The others, like Bouck, would walk.

Bouck leaned over James, who was lying on the floor. Barely conscious, James told the lieutenant, "Tell my mother when you get back that I love her, and I didn't suffer."

Bouck did not say a word. He simply squeezed the private's hand. Then he and the others who could walk were led out of the café and told to march. They headed east, toward Germany—and a prison camp.

Entering German territory, Bouck saw the string of defenses the Germans had set up, called the Siegfried Line. He also saw a line of tanks waiting

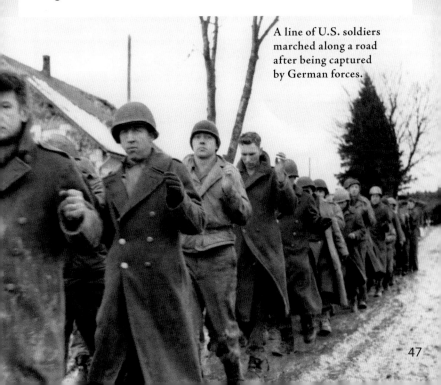

A line of U.S. soldiers marched along a road after being captured by German forces.

to head west into Belgium. Bouck realized that the German attack was much bigger than he had imagined back at the camp.

As snow fell, German soldiers riding on tanks pointed and laughed at the U.S. POWs. Then, one by one, the Americans were led to a German major, who questioned them. When Bouck met with the German officer, the major said, "You see all those tanks out there? And we have jet airplanes that will knock out your air corps. We have secret weapons that will end the war quickly. We'll be in Paris by Christmas. You'll go home, but not a winner."

U.S. Captain Dick Winters

Mourmelon, France,
December 17, 1944

Captain Dick Winters was enjoying a rare moment of calm. Since D-Day, he had seen plenty of action. His men in Easy Company, part of the U.S. 101st Airborne Division, had jumped into France that day, and they had been moving eastward ever since. They finally had a chance to rest when they reached Mourmelon. Now, as the end of the night approached, Winters learned the rest was over. Colonel Robert Sink told him that Easy Company would be moving out as soon as possible.

Winters knew his company was not ready for battle. They did not have much ammunition, and some of the men did not even have helmets. They also did not have the warm clothing they would need to fight in the winter. But they would be ready when the trucks came to take them to a new battle.

Captain Dick Winters

49

Military police officers guarded two German SS soldiers, who were captured behind Allied lines while disguised as U.S. soldiers.

4

GERMAN ADVANCE, ALLIED RESPONSE

Reports poured into General Eisenhower's
headquarters, and he now realized the size of the
German attack. While some U.S. units had put
up strong defenses, slowing the Germans, in other
areas along the front his troops were simply too
outnumbered to resist.

Eisenhower's office also received reports that some
Germans dressed as U.S. soldiers were in the Allied
lines and creating confusion. The staff also heard
rumors that teams of German assassins were on
their way to Paris to kill Eisenhower. The general's
security team would not take a chance. They moved
him to a new command post and increased the
guards for him and other top Allied generals.

That evening, Eisenhower sent a message to
General Omar Bradley and General Jacob Loucks
Devers, who commanded the 6th Army Group.
"The enemy is making a major thrust through

the Ardennes. My intention is to take immediate action to check the enemy advance; to launch a counter-offensive without delay with all forces north of the Moselle River."

German Sergeant Erich Michely

Near Bastendorf, Luxembourg,
December 18, 1944

Through the first two days of fighting, Sergeant Michely's division had made slow progress into Belgium. For Michely and his small gun crew, the traveling was even slower because they had to manage their horses over rough terrain. At times the men helped the animals pull the artillery.

Today was even harder for Michely and his men. With the fog and mist clearing somewhat, Allied planes had returned to the skies. Michely and the rest of the troops did not want to stay on the road too long, where they would be an easy target for Allied aircraft.

Near the town of Tandel, Luxembourg, Michely and his team were on a hill with other gun crews. They tried to find high ground so they could fire

A group of German soldiers walked past a line of burning U.S. military vehicles during the Battle of the Bulge.

down on the enemy. From the hill, they saw two U.S. tanks. The men armed their gun. One shell found its target, and a U.S. tank went up in flames. Then another gun team nearby fired at the second tank and destroyed it.

With the job done, Michely and his men set off again on their march through Luxembourg.

German Colonel Jochen Peiper

Trois-Ponts, Belgium,
December 18, 1944

After his initial successes the day before, Colonel Peiper and his tanks were meeting stiffer resistance from the Americans. Some Allied planes had been able to get into the air and attack his column. He had also lost more tanks battling the Americans at Stavelot, Belgium, though his division was able to keep moving. Peiper knew, though, that the longer it took him to reach the Meuse, the more reinforcements the Allies could put in place.

Peiper and his men reached Trois-Pont, Belgium. He wanted to cross a bridge there. Scouts brought good news—there was one still in place and strong enough to support the weight of his tanks. But he watched with anger as the bridge blew up in front of him, thanks to dynamite set off by U.S. Army engineers. Then there was another explosion, and another bridge nearby was gone.

Peiper directed his tanks to yet another bridge. As he led several tanks to the bridge, Peiper watched as this one, too, blew up, because of the U.S. dynamite. Peiper got out of his tank and hit his knee in anger. "The damned engineers!"

U.S. Captain Dick Winters

Outside Bastogne, Belgium,
December 19, 1944

The truck carrying Captain Winters, and some of his men, came to a stop. Since the day before, hundreds of trucks had carried the 101st Airborne Division to this area, where the Germans were closing in on Bastogne, Belgium. Whoever controlled the town, controlled the several major roads that passed through it. The Americans needed to hold on to it to stop the Germans from advancing farther.

Winters and his men jumped out of the truck. They could hear artillery fire coming from Bastogne. One paratrooper from the company said, "Here we go again!" Winters and his men were used to the sounds of battle.

As Easy Company began to march toward its new camp, U.S. troops that had been defending

Bastogne marched out. Some, though, were running, fear showing on their faces.

"Run, run," some of the retreating soldiers shouted. "They'll murder you, they'll kill you!"

Winters shook his head. He felt ashamed to think that U.S. soldiers could be so afraid.

"Got any ammo?" some of Winters's men asked the fleeing men. With Easy Company short on bullets, they could use all they could get. Then, like a gift from heaven, a lieutenant from another company drove up with ammunition and hand grenades. The men of Easy Company, and other companies, eagerly snatched up all they could.

As Winters and his men marched on, they saw that fierce fighting had gone on in the area. Passing through some woods, Winters saw the dead bodies of both German and U.S. troops. He knew his men and the rest of the 101st Airborne had to do all they could to keep the Germans from taking Bastogne.

U.S. General George S. Patton Jr.

Verdun, France,
December 19, 1944

General George S. Patton Jr. entered the school building that General Bradley was now using as a command post. They, along with General Eisenhower and other top Allied officers, were meeting to discuss the Allied strategy for halting the German attack and mounting their own counterattack.

Patton, the commander of the U.S. 3rd Army, was known as "Old Blood and Guts." Patton knew some people disliked him because he spoke his mind and challenged soldiers who seemed to be cowards. But he also knew he was a good general, after successfully leading troops across North Africa in 1942 and Sicily in 1943. He had taken command of the 3rd Army on August 1, 1944, and his forces had torn through German defenses in southern France. Only a shortage of supplies had kept him from racing into Germany before the other Allied armies reached that target.

U.S. General George S. Patton Jr.

After hearing an intelligence report from Major General Strong, Eisenhower discussed his desire to get troops to Bastogne as quickly as possible. The Germans were weaker there than farther to the north. A counterattack on the Germans's southern flank could begin to push them back. He asked Patton how soon he could send his men to the Ardennes to help stop the German advance.

"Three divisions in two days," Patton said simply.

His confident tone surprised the others in the room. Patton sensed they could not believe he could do it. Eisenhower said, "I want your initial blow to be a strong one! I'd even settle for the 23rd if it takes that long to get three full divisions."

In a few moments, Patton left the conference room and called his headquarters in Nancy, France. The other generals did not know that he had already made plans to send those troops north. With a simple code word to his office, the three divisions of the 3rd Army were ready to head out to Bastogne.

German Colonel Otto Skorzeny

Outside Malmedy, Belgium,
December 21, 1944

Colonel Skorzeny sat in the home he had seized to use as his headquarters. He could hear enemy shells whistling overhead, but the home was not in the line of fire. Although Hitler had ordered Skorzeny not to travel with his disguised commandos, he still had a role to play. Skorzeny was leading a German division that was now preparing to march on Malmedy, Belgium.

By now, Skorzeny had received more reports from the commandos behind enemy lines. Several reported success with cutting Allied communication lines and taking down signposts that would help the Americans find their way. Even more importantly, one team had found a huge supply of ammunition and blown it up. Several teams, though, had not reported. Skorzeny could only guess that they had been captured.

As daybreak approached, Skorzeny sent messages to several of his captains. He outlined his plan to

U.S. soldiers covered their ears as they shelled German positions with mortars.

overrun the enemy front lines and take Malmedy. But he also hoped to keep only a small force there. He wanted to push on and take control of the roads to the north.

Before he could launch his attack on Malmedy, Skorzeny heard artillery fire. The Americans had struck first, and soon he saw trucks bringing wounded men past his camp. The fighting went on all day.

That night Skorzeny was driving back from the division's headquarters when three enemy shells landed near his car. He jumped from the vehicle and took cover in a ditch. He felt something warm running down his face—blood! He had been hit by shrapnel. He returned to headquarters to have the wound treated. The doctor there wanted him to go to a hospital away from the action. Skorzeny refused—he wanted to go back to the front.

Augusta Chiwy

Bastogne, Belgium,
December 21, 1944

Augusta Chiwy felt the building shake as German artillery flew into Bastogne. She and several hundred townspeople had sought shelter in the basement of a Catholic school. They had been there for several days as the Germans had approached the town. Many civilians had fled Bastogne, but Chiwy, her father, and her aunt had stayed to help the sick and wounded.

Chiwy was a 23-year-old nurse who stood just 4 feet 8 inches tall. Less than a week before, on

December 16, she had traveled from Brussels, Belgium, to stay with her father for the Christmas holiday. Chiwy had been born in the Congo, in Africa, and her mother was black, while her father was white. Growing up, she had been the only mixed-race or black child in her class.

When she arrived in Bastogne, Chiwy had not yet heard that the Germans were attacking the Allies in Belgium. But now the Germans were closing in. In the cellar, the exploding shells stirred up dust, and the cries of the sick and injured filled the air. Chiwy tried to ignore all that and focus on helping as many people as she could.

Later that afternoon, when Chiwy was at her father's house, a U.S. military officer came to visit her. He tried to speak to her in English—which she knew a little bit of—and French, one of Belgium's two main languages. The officer said his name was Captain Jack Prior. He explained that he was a doctor and had set up an aid station in town to treat wounded soldiers. Another nurse working for him had told him about Chiwy. He asked if she would help him.

Chiwy saw the officer stare at her as he waited for her reply. She thought that he had a kind face.

Finally she said, "Oui," in French. Then, in English, she said, "Yes."

Chiwy followed Prior to the aid station. Even before she went in, a strong odor hit her. It was the smell of the dead and dying soldiers inside. She knew she would remember that smell for the rest of her life.

German Sergeant Erich Michely

Mertzig, Luxembourg,
December 22, 1944

Sergeant Michely rose early that morning. Over several days, he and the rest of Germany's 915th Regiment of the 352nd Division had passed through several towns. Now they were about to march into one called Mertzig, in Luxembourg.

Entering Mertzig, Michely saw that the town was deserted. He and his men left their artillery gun and horses in the street and went inside an empty hotel. The men went to the bar and helped themselves to drinks. Michely, though, had a strange feeling.

German soldiers ran past a burning tank as the Battle of the Bulge raged on.

He started to explore the building. At the back, Michely looked out and saw Allied troops advancing from a nearby hill. Then artillery shells began falling around the hotel. The sergeant went back to his men, and together they ran into the street. Several of their horses had already been killed in the shelling. Then enemy tanks appeared in the street.

"Take cover!" Michely yelled, but two of his men were still near their artillery gun. In a second, a blast from a U.S. tank destroyed the gun and killed his men.

Michely went back into the street. He and some of the men in the regiment managed to drag one gun up a small hill. They fired one shot, and the Americans replied with a blast of machine gun fire. Michely had never been under such intense fire before. When the shooting stopped for a moment, he and several other men ran into a nearby house. They heard the machine gun bullets ripping into the walls.

When the shooting stopped again, Michely went out of the house and toward the center of town. In the street he met a young officer named Clement, who demanded to know where Michely was going.

"My war is over," Michely said. "I intend to surrender to the Americans at the earliest and safest opportunity. You and the rest of the men should do the same."

Clement insisted that the men could still get away and rejoin the rest of the battalion.

Michely replied, "Where are we going to go? They'll shoot us like rabbits!"

Clement warned him that he would turn Michely in so he could be court-martialed for deserting his post.

Michely shook his head. "Before you can do that, you have to survive first."

Michely turned away and saw Clement and another soldier leave the street and start to cross a meadow. They made it only 35 yards before Michely saw Clement gunned down by the Americans. Now Michely was determined that this would be his last day of the war. He would find some Americans and surrender to them.

U.S. Captain Dick Winters

Near Foy, Belgium,
December 22, 1944

Captain Winters and his men sat shivering in the cold. About a foot of snow had fallen the day before. During the night, Winters had heard German artillery fire nearby. Now German snipers took occasional gunshots at Easy Company's position. The Americans still had artillery in Bastogne, Winters knew, but they were almost out of shells. They needed to save them for the huge German attack that was sure to come.

U.S. soldiers from the 7th Armored Division hunkered down in the snow as they advanced along a road near St. Vith, Belgium.

For now Winters, his men, and the rest of the 101st Airborne had one goal—to hold off the Germans until reinforcements came. Each side sent out patrols and exchanged gunfire, but no major fighting took place. The biggest challenge for

Winters now was keeping his men warm, fed, and ready to fight. The men ate packaged K-rations. If the cooks made a hot meal, it was cold by the time it reached the men. And Winters saw several soldiers develop trench foot, a disease that results when feet are cold and wet for too long.

Winters knew that sometimes soldiers got so depressed by such conditions that they would shoot themselves in the foot. Then they could be sent back to France and, eventually, home. But Winters knew his men would take the tough conditions and do their duty.

U.S. troops trudged through the snow as they made their way through the Ardennes forest.

A DIFFICULT CHRISTMAS SEASON

Waking early, General Patton received word that the first of his troops were marching on Bastogne. By now he had moved his headquarters to the capital of tiny Luxembourg. From there, he followed the progress of the three divisions he had promised Eisenhower. As snow fell, their advance was slower than Patton had hoped for. But at least they were making progress.

Before the battle, Patton had visited his troops to prepare them for the fighting to come. He had made a point of jumping in a jeep and driving along the roads his men took to reach Bastogne. He wanted them to know that he appreciated the difficult conditions they faced.

Patton received reports throughout the day about the fighting going on around Bastogne. The 101st Airborne fought off one German attack. In some areas, the Germans were waiting for Patton's forces and managed to hold them off. When the day ended, Patton wrote in his diary, "I am satisfied but not particularly happy over the results today."

The next morning, however, Patton and the other U.S. generals received good news. The weather was finally clearing. Now hundreds of Allied planes could take to the skies. Some would drop supplies to the U.S. troops in Bastogne. Others would go for German tanks and artillery that circled the town, as well as attack German air bases.

U.S. Lieutenant Lyle Bouck

On a train in Germany, December 23, 1944

Lieutenant Bouck and the other men, who had been crammed into the railway car, shivered in the cold. They had started their journey to a POW camp several days before. All Bouck and the others had to eat were a few pieces of bread. Bouck's stomach tightened in pain, and his wounded leg throbbed. As the train rumbled on, the men took turns sleeping on the bare wooden floor. Meanwhile, a pile of their waste grew larger in a corner of the car.

As evening approached, the train stopped. The men inside could hear the sound of warplanes approaching—British warplanes. A lead plane dropped a flare to light up the targets below. Bouck heard the explosion from a bomb, and then another. He felt the car shake as one bomb hit farther up the train. Then the car toppled on its side, sending men sprawling everywhere. The blast did not hurt Bouck, but he was sure other Americans had been killed. When the bombing raid ended, the Germans fixed the tracks and got the train moving again. Bouck was once again heading deeper into Germany.

German Colonel Jochen Peiper

La Gleize, Belgium,
December 24, 1944

Just after midnight, Colonel Peiper gave the message to his officers that they would have to pull back—and soon. Peiper had known for several days that he could not reach the Meuse River, as Adolf Hitler had hoped. Although by the end of December 19 he had taken the towns of La Gleize, Stoumont, and Cheneux, he knew the Americans were getting stronger. They had held off his advance, retaken a town he had already captured, and blown up a bridge that his men needed to cross to get supplies. Peiper had radioed to General Wilhelm Mohnke that he was quickly running out of fuel.

For several days, the Americans had continued to close in on Peiper and his tanks. He had moved many of his forces to La Gleize and set up a headquarters there. But now he knew he could not stay in the village. Mohnke had sent a message the day before saying he could not send more fuel or ammunition.

Peiper told his men to prepare to withdraw without their tanks and artillery. He outlined his plan: The wounded would stay in La Gleize so the Americans could help them. A few other men would stay behind to blow up the tanks and other equipment. The rest of the division would leave.

In the dark, the men broke up into small groups and headed out of the village. Peiper had only 800 of his 5,000 men left, not counting the 300 or so wounded troops he was leaving behind. With luck they would reach the safety of the German lines. But Peiper knew that their Watch on the Rhine was over.

U.S. Captain Dick Winters

Outside Bastogne, Belgium,
December 24, 1944

The morning silence on the day of Christmas Eve was broken when German snipers began firing at Easy Company. Winters and his men fought off the attack, which continued through the morning. When the shooting stopped, Sergeant Carwood Lipton went out to count the enemy dead. He reported that 38 had been killed.

That afternoon, Winters and the others gathered to hear a Christmas message from their commander, Brigadier General Anthony McAuliffe. In it, McAuliffe explained how the German commander

A U.S. soldier blended in with his surroundings as he took aim at enemy forces.

had sent a message on December 22 asking him to surrender. McAuliffe had replied: "To the German commander: NUTS!"

Winters was glad to hear that McAuliffe would not back down. He was proud to serve under the general, even as he and the rest of Easy Company knew they faced tough fighting ahead.

Augusta Chiwy

Bastogne, Belgium,
December 24, 1944, 8:30 p.m.

The last several days had been hard ones for Nurse Chiwy. The other volunteer nurse, Renée Lemaire, was easily sickened by the sight of blood. So when Dr. Prior had to amputate a soldier's foot, Chiwy assisted the doctor and tried to calm the fearful patient. All Prior had for tools was an army knife. All they could give the soldier to kill the pain was some alcohol. After the doctor removed the foot, Chiwy quickly applied medicine to prevent an infection and sewed up the wound.

Now it was 8:30 p.m. on Christmas Eve. Dr. Prior and another officer motioned to Chiwy. They wanted her to join them in the house next door to drink some champagne they had found. Chiwy hesitated at first, not wanting to leave the patients alone. But then she went with the men to celebrate the holiday.

Next door, Dr. Prior was just about to pour the drinks when they all heard a loud whistling noise. It was followed by an explosion that blew out the windows and sent Chiwy flying through a glass wall. Out on the street, she picked herself up and checked to see if she was injured. Luckily, she only had some minor cuts and bruises. But when she looked around, she saw that a German bomb had destroyed the aid station where she and Prior worked—and where dozens of wounded men had been resting.

Bastogne, Belgium, lay in ruins after the Germans's bombings.

It took Chiwy and Dr. Prior just a few seconds to see that all the men, who had been on the first floor, were now dead. But from the basement they heard the screams of some men who had survived. With bombs still falling, Chiwy and Dr. Prior tended to these men on the street. Soon the men were taken to an army hospital outside of town.

General Dwight D. Eisenhower

Paris, France,
December 25, 1944

General Eisenhower felt like a prisoner in his own headquarters. The fears that German soldiers were lurking behind enemy lines had grown. The general's security team believed his life could be in danger, so it limited Eisenhower's movements.

Today he was supposed to have hosted a large holiday feast. Now he instead ate with just a few officers. His mood was not the best. Intelligence reports said that Hitler was likely to keep up with the offensive.

But Eisenhower saw some good signs. Although the Germans had carried out the surprise attack, they were not as well equipped as the Allies. U.S. and British planes were inflicting heavy damage, and General Patton would soon be in Bastogne. Finally, almost 10 days into the battle, the Germans had not reached the Meuse River, which was obviously their goal. Hitler might keep attacking, but the Allies were in a good position to hold off the Nazis.

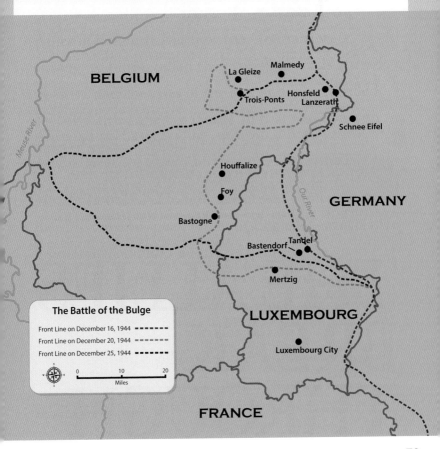

BELGIUM

La Gleize
Malmedy
Trois-Ponts
Honsfeld
Lanzerath
Schnee Eifel

Meuse River

Houffalize

Foy

Bastogne

Our River

GERMANY

Tandel
Bastendorf
Mertzig

The Battle of the Bulge

Front Line on December 16, 1944 ----
Front Line on December 20, 1944 ----
Front Line on December 25, 1944 ----

0   10   20
Miles

LUXEMBOURG

Luxembourg City

FRANCE

Adolf Hitler (second from right) met with several Nazi leaders and Italian leader Benito Mussolini (far right).

THE ALLIES BREAK THROUGH

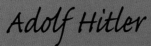

In his bunker, Adolf Hitler was
meeting with several of his officers,
including General Heinz Guderian.
The general had doubted the ability to
achieve Hitler's aims with Watch on
the Rhine. Now he told Hitler about
his concerns in the east. Soviet forces
were strong along the Vistula River in
Poland. With the attack in the west
failing, Guderian thought Hitler should
pull men from Belgium and move
them east.

Hitler looked at the reports that
Guderian had laid out on the table.
"Who is responsible for producing this
rubbish?!" he said.

Hitler refused to believe that
the Soviet army was so strong along

the Vistula. And he still thought his forces could achieve their goals in the west.

In fact, Hitler wanted to launch a new attack in the west, beginning on New Year's Eve. Some German troops would strike at Alsace-Lorraine, France. Hitler figured an attack there would force Eisenhower to move troops out of the Ardennes. Hitler called this new attack Operation Nordwind.

The generals looked at each other but did not say anything. Hitler would run the war the way he wanted—even if it led to defeat.

U.S. General George S. Patton Jr.

Luxembourg City, Luxembourg,
December 26, 1944, 2 p.m.

Despite reports that the 4th Armored Division was closing in on Bastogne, General Patton was concerned. He thought his men should have reached the town by now, but the Germans were still counterattacking.

At 2 p.m., Patton received a call from General Hugh Gaffey, who commanded the division. He believed several battalions could break through and reach Bastogne.

U.S. soldiers from the 101st Airborne Division marched along a road on the outskirts of Bastogne, Belgium.

"Try it," Patton said.

By that evening, Patton received the good news that the 4th Armored Division had reached the center of Bastogne. Although the Germans still surrounded the city on three sides, the Americans were now prepared to attack the enemy.

U.S. Captain Dick Winters

Outside Bastogne, Belgium,
December 26, 1944

Captain Winters watched with relief as ambulances reached the 101st Airborne and began taking the wounded to field hospitals. The ambulances were a sure sign of what he and Easy Company had just learned: the 4th Armored Division had busted through part of the German lines around Bastogne. Winters considered this news the best Christmas present ever, even if it came a day late.

Now trucks began rolling toward the lines, bringing food and supplies. The men saw their first newspapers in weeks too. Winters and the others read that back in the United States people thought the soldiers of the 101st Airborne were heroes for holding off the Germans.

And now, Winters thought, with any luck the arrival of General Patton's men might mean that Easy Company could go back to its base in France.

Augusta Chiwy

Heintz Barracks Hospital, Bastogne, Belgium, December 26, 1944

Augusta Chiwy dressed the wounds of injured soldiers. The fighting around Bastogne was heavy, and Dr. Prior, once again, needed all the help he could get.

U.S. troops used jeeps to carry wounded solders away from battle in the Ardennes region of Belgium.

Earlier, Chiwy had not been sure she could do this difficult work again, after what had happened on Christmas Eve. After the bombing of the aid station, Chiwy had gone back to her father's basement. Sitting alone, she began to cry as she thought about all the soldiers who had been killed. Renée Lemaire had also died in the blast.

Eventually, though, Chiwy had gone back to the site of the destruction. There, she had run into Dr. Prior. He explained that he was now working at the hospital at General McAuliffe's headquarters. There were still many men who needed medical attention. Chiwy decided she would help the doctor.

So now Chiwy was, once again, doing her part to help in the battle against the Germans.

Adolf Hitler

Eagle's Eyrie, Ziegenberg, Germany, December 27, 1944

Hitler studied the reports from his generals in the field. The Americans had reached Bastogne with a sizable force, and more were sure to come. He received a message from Field Marshals Rundstedt and Model. If the Germans had any hope of reaching the Meuse River, they had to beat Patton in Bastogne. Hitler gave his approval for a newly arrived Panzer corps to lead a major assault on the U.S. forces around Bastogne. Hitler wrote, "The enemy wedge into Bastogne under all circumstances must be destroyed."

Lieutenant Colonel Otto Skorzeny

Eagle's Eyrie, Ziegenberg, Germany, December 31, 1944

Lieutenant Colonel Skorzeny waited for Adolf Hitler in a small room at the leader's temporary headquarters. When Hitler entered, he noticed Skorzeny's wound. Hitler called for his personal doctor to examine the injury. The doctor came in and took Skorzeny to an operating room where he treated Skorzeny's eye.

By the afternoon, Skorzeny was with Hitler again.

"We are now going to start a great offensive in the southeast," Hitler said as he told Skorzeny about Operation Nordwind.

Skorzeny was surprised to hear this and to see Hitler so cheerful. The Ardennes offensive had failed. Yet seeing Hitler's mood helped cheer up Skorzeny too. Soon he would return to action.

U.S. soldiers from the 101st Engineers walked through the snow-covered forest after a battle with German forces near Wiltz, Luxembourg.

THE PATH TO VICTORY

Captain Winters watched it snow again and listened to more artillery fire. He had not gotten his wish to go back to France. Instead, he and Easy Company were still fighting Germans in the woods of Belgium.

Winters had received orders that morning to move his men to cover territory previously held by another battalion. The Americans had kept the Germans out of Bastogne, but the enemy was still in the area, still trying to weaken the Americans as much as possible.

As Easy Company moved out, the Germans unleashed a huge artillery assault. Winters and the men dove for any cover they could find. Some jumped into old foxholes. Others took cover in the holes in the ground created by earlier German shelling. Finally the assault stopped, but not before two of the company's sergeants were badly wounded.

That night, Winters sat in his foxhole. Ice frosted the walls of his tiny shelter. He thought about the day's battle and all that Easy Company had faced. It had lost half its men since reaching Belgium. Among the losses were several experienced leaders whom the troops trusted. Winters sensed that the men's spirits were low. But he knew Easy Company would keep doing its best.

U.S. Lieutenant Lyle Bouck

Nuremberg, Germany,
January 3, 1945

On the edge of Nuremberg, Germany, Lieutenant Bouck thrust his shovel in the ground and dug up another bit of dirt. He had arrived at a POW camp outside the city several days before. All through the night of January 2, he and the other POWs heard Allied planes bomb Nuremberg.

Now, with the morning light, the Germans had ordered the men to go to work. Some POWs looked for and moved the dead. Others, like Bouck, dug graves for German civilians who had died in the attack. All around he could see the ruins of what had been homes and businesses. Some of the dead bodies barely looked human because of the intense heat of the fires that had charred them.

A German civilian watched as Bouck dug the graves. The work was made harder by the injury to his leg, which still had not healed. Bouck watched as the German went back to what was left of the man's home. He returned in a few minutes holding a can. With gestures he told Bouck that the medicine inside would help treat his leg. Bouck took the can and said, "Danke"—which is "Thank you" in German.

General Dwight D. Eisenhower

Paris, France,
January 9, 1945

General Eisenhower opened the telegram he had just received from British leader Winston Churchill. The two had met almost a week before at Eisenhower's headquarters. Eisenhower had told Churchill that the Allies needed Soviet troops to attack the Germans in the east. Churchill had said he would ask Soviet leader Joseph Stalin to take action to help the Allies fighting in the Ardennes.

Now, in the telegram in front of him, Eisenhower read the message Churchill had sent Stalin: "The battle in the west is very heavy. . . . It is Eisenhower's great desire and need to know in outline what you plan to do, as this obviously affects all his and our major decisions."

Soviet leader Joseph Stalin

Eisenhower then read Stalin's reply. The weather was currently too bad for the Soviets to launch a major attack. But Stalin promised that one would come in the second half of January. The Soviet leader wrote, "You may rest assured that we shall do everything possible to render assistance to the glorious forces of our Allies."

Eisenhower was glad to get this news. Even though his men were attacking the German bulge from both the north and the south, he welcomed help. Once the Soviet troops started fighting again, Hitler would have to move men out of the Ardennes to fight in the east. Eisenhower knew that would make his job much easier.

Adolf Hitler

Eagle's Eyrie, Ziegenberg, Germany,
January 9, 1945

Adolf Hitler sat in his bunker and thought about what he should do next. The last few days had been difficult ones. Hitler realized the Ardennes offensive was crumbling. From his generals in the field, he had learned that the U.S. 1st and 3rd armies were closing in on the German salient, or the outward bulge in their front line. And the Allied air attacks were continuing to cause heavy damage to bridges that Germany relied on to move troops and supplies to the front. Field Marshal Walther Model had said the day before that Hitler should pull troops out of the salient before they were trapped. Hitler had reluctantly agreed.

Now he made another decision. He instructed his generals to pull back some of the tank divisions. They would still be available later to fight the advancing Allies. But Hitler realized his grand plan for a last successful offensive had failed. He would soon lose the Battle of the Bulge.

U.S. Captain Dick Winters

Outside Foy, Belgium,
January 12, 1945, 9 a.m.

Captain Winters addressed two of his lieutenants and told them to prepare Easy Company for an attack on the village of Foy, Belgium.

The men set out at 9 a.m., and Winters watched them advance. Machine gunners on the side covered

U.S. soldiers advanced across a vast field near Bastogne, Belgium.

the main part of Easy Company as it crossed an open field toward the village. Suddenly the men led by Lieutenant Norman Dike stopped in the field.

Our men are like a bunch of sitting ducks, Winters thought as he tried to contact Dike by radio. The lieutenant did not reply. Then Winters heard Colonel Sink call out to him, "What are you going to do, Winters?"

"I'm going!" Winters replied as he grabbed his rifle and ran out to take command of the company. But then he stopped—Winters realized it was more important for him to command the whole battalion and not just Easy Company. He instructed Lieutenant Ronald Speirs, who was standing nearby, to go out and take over for Dike. Winters watched as Speirs ran across the field, took over for Dike, and then ran out again to contact another company nearby. Meanwhile, German artillery fired away at the Americans. Winters watched as the men made their way into Foy.

At 11 a.m., Winters received good news. His men had taken the village, along with 20 prisoners. Easy Company had lost just one man in the fighting.

U.S. General George S. Patton Jr.

Outside Houffalize, Belgium, January 15, 1945

General Patton left his headquarters and drove out toward Houffalize, Belgium, to see some of the fighting for himself. For three days, his men had slowly advanced toward the town. It was where his 3rd Army and the 1st Army under Field Marshal Bernard Montgomery were supposed to meet.

Earlier that morning, Patton had received good news. A squadron of his men had made contact with an infantry unit from the 1st Army in Houffalize. The Germans had already left the heavily bombed-out town. The successful drive had been costly to Patton's 11th Armored Division, which had led the charge into Houffalize. It had lost 32 tanks and suffered more than 400 casualties since December 13.

Now, as he drove in the viciously cold weather, Patton noticed a dead German machine gunner. His body had frozen almost instantly, and his outstretched arms still held a belt of ammunition. Both sides had paid a high price in the battle for Houffalize. But the men in Patton's division had done their job.

General Dwight D. Eisenhower

Paris, France,
January 18, 1945

At his headquarters, General Eisenhower continued to make plans for the Allies's advance into Germany. With the joining of his two armies in Houffalize and the Germans's continuing retreat, General Eisenhower and the Allies had won the Battle of the Bulge. And in the east, the Soviet Union had resumed its attack on German forces. That day, he wrote to tell his top generals that the Germans had suffered "severe losses in men and materiel."

Still, Eisenhower knew that the Germans had been able to pull out many men and weapons and were still a powerful enemy. As he made plans to go on the attack again, Eisenhower also wanted to make sure he defended the territory the Allies held. But he also told his generals, "My intention is to regain the strategical initiative by launching strong offensives north of the Moselle."

Eisenhower explained that he wanted to begin the offensives as soon as possible. With luck and skill, the Allies would soon defeat Hitler and the Nazis once and for all.

U.S. tanks and troops continued to march eastward through the Ardennes forest toward Nazi Germany.

EPILOGUE

The Allies paid a high price for their victory in the Ardennes. The United States—alone—lost 19,000 men, and more than 47,000 were wounded. The Germans also destroyed hundreds of Allied tanks. But German losses were even higher. Total casualties were between 80,000 and 100,000, including more than 12,000 killed, and Allied planes dropped more than 100,000 tons of bombs on German targets.

Among the Americans killed were several hundred prisoners. Soldiers in Colonel Peiper's Panzer division murdered some of them as Peiper's main force headed to Malmedy, Belgium. This was later called the Malmedy Massacre. Other U.S. POWs and Belgian civilians were also killed by Peiper's SS troops during the Battle of the Bulge. Historians have argued over whether Peiper ordered or knew about these killings.

By February 1945, the Allies had recaptured almost all of the ground they had lost in December. But despite the loss in the Ardennes and the

U.S. soldiers lined up for rations during the Battle of the Bulge.

advancing Soviet troops, Hitler kept fighting. By now generals on both sides knew the war would end soon. The Allied victory would come when their troops reached Berlin, if Hitler did not surrender first.

Through the late winter and spring, many of the Allied troops that had taken part in the Battle of the Bulge continued moving eastward. Eisenhower wanted to inflict heavy damage on the German troops west of the Rhine River. That way, they could not take part in a defense of Berlin once the Allies crossed the river. A major offensive at different spots along the Rhine began in early February. By late March, Allied troops were crossing the river. Meanwhile, Allied bombing raids continued to destroy vital German targets, especially fuel supplies.

As they fought, more Allied troops and supplies poured into Europe. By March, General Eisenhower had almost 4 million soldiers under his command. In the east, some 2 million Soviet troops faced just 400,000 Germans. As the Allies advanced on Berlin from two sides, Adolf Hitler killed himself on April 30, 1945. On May 7, the remaining members of the German government announced their surrender. World War II in Europe was over. By mid-August, Japan had surrendered as well.

U.S. troops from the 82nd Airborne Division marched through the snow near Heersbach, Belgium.

After the war, some of the German officers who took part in the Battle of the Bulge were put on trial for war crimes. Colonel Jochen Peiper was sentenced to death for his alleged role in the Malmedy Massacre, but later his sentence was reduced, and he served time in prison.

Lieutenant Colonel Otto Skorzeny managed to escape the Allies and settled in Spain. Many common soldiers returned to their civilian lives in Germany.

On the U.S. side, General Dwight D. Eisenhower was elected president of the United States in 1952. He held the office for eight years.

Lieutenant Lyle Bouck was freed from a German POW camp at the end of April 1945. He became a chiropractor. In 1966, he received a medal for his actions during the Battle of the Bulge.

Captain Dick Winters eventually earned the rank of major. After the war, he became a successful businessman. Winters died in 2011, but one year later a monument dedicated to combat leadership was raised in his name near Utah Beach in Normandy, France. Atop the monument is a likeness of Winters leading his men into battle.

Captain Dick Winters's statue stands atop a monument in France dedicated to combat leadership during the D-Day invasion.

In Belgium, Augusta Chiwy left nursing for a time, but later returned to that career. Her role during the Battle of the Bulge was mostly forgotten until a historian named Martin King learned about her. In 2007, he found her living in a rest home outside Brussels and made a film about her life.

The Battle of the Bulge is remembered today as the largest battle ever fought by the U.S. Army. It marked a huge gamble by Hitler as he tried to catch the Allies by surprise. That part of his plan worked, which let his forces create the "bulge" in his enemy's line. But the Allies had many advantages that Hitler could not match. The Battle of the Bulge slowed Eisenhower's plans for defeating Germany, but it did not crush them.

Augusta Chiwy met with U.S. Ambassador to Belgium Denise Campbell Bauer in 2014.

TIMELINE

SEPTEMBER 1, 1939: German leader Adolf Hitler sends his troops into Poland, starting World War II.

DECEMBER 7, 1941: Japan's attack on the naval base at Pearl Harbor, in Hawaii, brings the United States into World War II.

DECEMBER 1943: General Dwight D. Eisenhower takes command of all Allied troops in Europe.

JUNE 6, 1944: Allied forces land on the beaches of Normandy, France, to fight the Germans in what became known as D-Day.

SEPTEMBER 1944: Hitler begins making plans to attack the Allies.

DECEMBER 16, 1944: The Germans begin Watch on the Rhine and attack Allied forces in the Ardennes in Belgium and Luxembourg.

DECEMBER 17, 1944: Eisenhower begins rushing the 101st and 82nd Airborne Divisions to the front to help the soldiers under attack.

DECEMBER 19, 1944: Eisenhower agrees to send three divisions of General George S. Patton Jr.'s 3rd Army to attack the Germans in Bastogne, Belgium.

DECEMBER 22, 1944: The first of Patton's troops reach the edge of Bastogne.

DECEMBER 26, 1944: Hitler announces plans for a second attack, called Operation Nordwind, in Alsace-Lorraine, France; Patton's troops enter the center of Bastogne.

DECEMBER 30, 1944: Reporter Larry Newman refers to the German advance in the Ardennes as a bulge, leading to the name Battle of the Bulge.

JANUARY 8–9, 1945: Hitler orders some troops out of the Ardennes, with some going to fight the Russians in Poland.

JANUARY 16, 1945: Troops of the U.S. 1st and 3rd Armies meet in Houffalize, Belgium, effectively ending the German offensive.

APRIL 30, 1945: Hitler kills himself in Berlin, Germany.

MAY 7, 1945: Germany surrenders to the Allies.

AUGUST 6, 1945: The United States drops an atomic bomb on Hiroshima, Japan, then drops a second bomb on the city of Nagasaki three days later.

AUGUST 14, 1945: Japan announces it will surrender, ending World War II.

GLOSSARY

Allies (AL-lyz)—a group of countries, including the United States, England, and France, that fought together in World War II

artillery (ar-TIL-uh-ree)—large guns, such as cannons or missile launchers, that require several soldiers to load, aim, and fire

bunker (BUHNG-kuhr)—an underground shelter from bomb attacks and gunfire

casualty (KAZH-oo-uhl-tee)—someone who is injured, captured, killed, or missing in an accident, a disaster, or a war

commando (kuh-MAN-doh)—specially trained soldiers who make quick, destructive raids on enemy territory

flank (FLANGK)—the far left or right side of a group of soldiers, a fort, or a naval fleet

front (FRUNT)—a military line formed by the farthest-advanced combat units

infantry (IN-fuhn-tree)—a group of people in the military trained to fight on land

intelligence (in-TEL-uh-jenss)—information about an enemy's plans or actions

K-ration (KAY RASH-uhn)—cold, packaged food given to U.S. soldiers that included canned meat, biscuits, and chocolate bars

materiel (muh-tihr-EE-ehl)—military materials and equipment

reinforcements (ree-in-FORSS-muhnts)—extra troops sent into battle

salient (SAL-yuhnt)—a line of defense that projects farthest toward the enemy

shrapnel (SHRAP-huhl)—pieces that have broken off from an explosive shell

Soviet Union (SOH-vee-et YOON-yuhn)—a former federation of 15 republics that included Russia, Ukraine, and other nations of eastern Europe and northern Asia; also called the Union of Soviet Socialist Republics (USSR)

SS (ESS-ESS)—the Nazi special police force made up of Hitler's bodyguards; the SS also ran the Nazi concentration camps

CRITICAL THINKING QUESTIONS

1. A number of Adolf Hitler's trusted military officers and advisors expressed concerns about the potential success of his Watch on the Rhine offensive. Why do you think Hitler went through with the attack anyway? Do you think the war would have ended differently if he hadn't launched the attack? Why?

2. Augusta Chiwy put herself in great danger to help others while Bastogne was under attack. Why do you think she was willing to do so?

3. General Patton's nickname was "Old Blood and Guts." Based on his actions during the Battle of the Bulge, what characteristics do you think he displayed to earn this nickname? Why do you think these characteristics served him well as a military leader in World War II?

INTERNET SITES

The Battle of the Bulge
https://encyclopedia.ushmm.org/content/en/article/battle-of-the-bulge

Dwight D. Eisenhower Presidential Library, Museum, and Boyhood Home
https://www.eisenhower.archives.gov

World War II: The Fall of Nazi Germany
https://www.theatlantic.com/photo/2011/10/world-war-ii-the-fall-of-nazi-germany/100166

FURTHER READING

Altman, Linda Jacobs. *Adolf Hitler and the Rise of the Third Reich.* People and Events That Changed the World. New York: Enslow Publishing, 2016.

Atkinson, Rick, and Kate Waters. *Battle of the Bulge.* New York: Henry Holt, 2015.

Hatch, Alden. *General George Patton: Old Blood and Guts.* Sterling Point. Minneapolis: Voyageur Press, 2017.

Marsico, Katie. *World War II: Why They Fought.* What They Were Fighting For. North Mankato, MN: Compass Point Books, 2016.

Summers, Elizabeth. *Weapons and Vehicles of World War II.* Tools of War. North Mankato, MN: Capstone Press, 2016.

SELECTED BIBLIOGRAPHY

Ambrose, Stephen E. *Band of Brothers: E Company, 506th Regiment, 101st Airborne, from Normandy to Hitler's Eagle's Nest.* New York: Simon & Schuster, 2001.

Astor, Gerald. *A Blood-Dimmer Tide: The Battle of the Bulge by the Men Who Fought It.* New York: Donald I. Fine, 1992.

Bergstrom, Christer. *The Ardennes 1944–1945: Hitler's Winter Offensive.* Havertown, PA: Casemate Publishers, 2014.

Caddick-Adams, Peter. *Snow and Steel: The Battle of the Bulge, 1944–1945.* New York: Oxford University Press, 2015.

Delaforce, Patrick. *The Battle of the Bulge: Hitler's Final Gamble.* Harlow, Eng.: Pearson Education Limited, 2004.

Hirshson, Stanley P. *General Patton: A Soldier's Life.* New York: HarperCollins, 2002.

Kershaw, Alex. *The Longest Winter: The Battle of the Bulge and the Epic Story of World War II's Most Decorated Platoon.* Cambridge, MA: Da Capo Press, 2004.

Mitcham, Samuel W. Jr. *Panzers in Winter: Hitler's Army and the Battle of the Bulge.* Westport, CT: Praeger Security International, 2006.

Neill, George. *Infantry Soldier: Holding the Line at the Battle of the Bulge.* Norman, OK: University of Oklahoma Press, 2000.

Parker, Danny S., ed. *Hitler's Ardennes Offensive: The German View of the Battle of the Bulge.* London: Greenhill Books, 1997.

Rickard, John Nelson. *Advance and Destroy: Patton as Commander in the Bulge.* Lexington: University Press of Kentucky, 2011.

INDEX

ABOUT THE AUTHOR

Michael Burgan is a freelance writer who specializes in books for children and young adults, both fiction and nonfiction. A graduate of the University of Connecticut with a degree in history, Burgan is also a produced playwright and the editor of *The Biographer's Craft*, the newsletter for Biographers International Organization. He lives in Santa Fe, New Mexico.